PATHWAY BIBLE GUIDES

Jesus Through Old Testament Eyes

BY MATTHEW JENSEN

Jesus Through Old Testament Eyes
Pathway Bible Guides
© Matthias Media 2013

Matthias Media
(St Matthias Press Ltd ACN 067 558 365)
PO Box 225
Kingsford NSW 2032
Australia
Telephone: (02) 9233 4627; international: +61 2 9233 4627
Email: info@matthiasmedia.com.au
Internet: www.matthiasmedia.com.au

Matthias Media (USA)
Telephone: 330 953 1702; international: +1 330 953 1702
Email: sales@matthiasmedia.com
Internet: www.matthiasmedia.com

ISBN 978 1 922206 03 9

Cover design and typesetting by Matthias Media.
Series concept design by Lankshear Design.

CONTENTS

BEFORE YOU BEGIN

These studies investigate how the New Testament uses the Old Testament to present the gospel of Jesus. It traces how the significance of the events of Jesus' life, death, resurrection and present rule can only be properly understood when viewed through the glasses of the Old Testament.

There are eight studies in all. The first study outlines the general method to be followed: because the apostles used the Old Testament to interpret the significance of the events of Jesus' life, death, resurrection and present rule, they have provided us with an example and a pattern that we should follow. The seven studies that follow work through the events of Jesus' life systematically, demonstrating that the use of the Old Testament is crucial to understanding these events.

As the Bible (not to mention the world around us) shows, Jesus' life can be (and often is) badly misunderstood. But, thankfully, the coming of God's Son did not occur in a vacuum. God had graciously been preparing the way for many hundreds of years, through the events and prophecies recorded in the pages of the Old Testament. When the Old Testament sets the parameters for understanding the life, death and resurrection of Jesus, we can have enormous clarity and confidence that we have rightly understood the life and ministry of our Saviour.

It is my prayer that these studies will help you to see the glory of the Lord Jesus Christ more clearly as you see him presented "in accordance with the Scriptures" (I Cor 15:3-4).

Matthew Jensen
November 2012

1. UNDERSTANDING JESUS

 **Getting started**

For Jews demand signs and Greeks seek wisdom, but we preach Christ crucified, a stumbling block to Jews and folly to Gentiles, but to those who are called, both Jews and Greeks, Christ the power of God and the wisdom of God. (1 Cor 1:22-24)

Why do you think there are so many different views about Jesus? What is at stake if the identity of Jesus is misunderstood?

☀ Light from the Word

Read 1 Corinthians 15:1-8.

1. What four events in Jesus' life make up Paul's gospel? Why might it have been necessary for Paul to "remind" the Corinthians of these things?

2. What is the meaning or purpose of Jesus' death?

3. Why can Paul be sure that Jesus' death was for sins?

4. What are "the Scriptures" that Paul refers to as explaining the significance of Jesus' death and resurrection?

5. How are the Corinthians saved?

Read Luke 24:13-49.

6. Why don't the two disciples recognize Jesus as they walk with him?

7. What does Jesus do for the disciples to help them understand what he had just done? What impact does this have on them?

8. What similarities can you see between Luke's account and Paul's presentation of the gospel in 1 Corinthians 15?

 ## To finish

What should we use to understand Jesus' death and resurrection correctly? How will this help us to avoid misunderstandings about Jesus? What is the danger in misunderstanding Jesus?

 ## Give thanks and pray

- Give thanks to God for the gospel that saves—the gospel of Jesus' death for sins and resurrection to life.
- Ask God to help you correctly understand the gospel events in light of the Old Testament, and to enable you to hold on to the gospel and not go elsewhere.

2. THE HISTORY AND EXPECTATIONS OF ISRAEL

 **Getting started**

> They are Israelites, and to them belong the adoption, the glory, the covenants, the giving of the law, the worship, and the promises. To them belong the patriarchs, and from their race, according to the flesh, is the Christ who is God over all, blessed forever. Amen. (Rom 9:4-5)

What expectations of the future do you hold for your nation? Why do you have these expectations?

⚙ Light from the Word

Read Matthew 1:1-17.

1. Who are the two greatest and most significant men in Israel's history that Jesus stands in line with? From your knowledge of the Bible, why are they considered so important?

2. What other significant event in the life of Israel does Matthew also highlight?

Read Matthew 1:18-25.

3. Who is Jesus born to?

4. According to Matthew, why is Jesus born in this particular way?

Read Matthew 2:1-12.

5. Where is Jesus born, and why?

Read Matthew 2:13-15.

6. Why does Joseph take Jesus and Mary to Egypt?

7. Matthew tells us that this fulfilled a prophecy from Hosea 11:1, which originally described Israel's exodus from slavery in Egypt. What does this tell us about the way that Jesus sometimes fulfils Old Testament prophecy?

Read Matthew 2:16-18.

8. Why does Herod kill the male children in and around Bethlehem?

Read Matthew 2:19-23.

9. Where does Joseph decide to live after returning from Egypt? Why does this decision matter?

 To finish

List the ways that Jesus' birth fulfilled the plans of God and the expectations of Israel. Why is this pattern of promise and fulfilment so important?

 Give thanks and pray

Thank God for his plan to save humanity through Jesus—a plan that covered thousands of years and fulfilled all his promises to the people of Israel.

3. ABRAHAM: THE FATHER OF ISRAEL

 Getting started

The book of the genealogy of Jesus Christ, the son of David, the son of Abraham... So all the generations from Abraham to David were fourteen generations, and from David to the deportation to Babylon fourteen generations, and from the deportation to Babylon to the Christ fourteen generations. (Matt 1:1, 17)

Do you have any (in)famous people in your family history? If so, who? How does being related to this person affect you?

☀ Light from the Word

Read Genesis 12:1-3.

1. List the promises God makes to Abraham.

2. From your knowledge of the Bible, how does God fulfil these promises?

3. Think back to the previous study. When Jesus is born, what is the state of the fulfilment of these promises?

4. Why would being a 'child of Abraham' have been so important to an ancient Israelite?

Read Galatians 3:5-14.

5. How does someone become a child of Abraham, a member of God's promised great nation?

6. This passage sets up a contrast between blessing and curse. What group of people does Paul describe as "cursed"? Why would this have come as a surprise to some of Paul's readers?

7. What is the blessing that Abraham's children receive?

8. How are the Gentiles (or nations) blessed and included in God's promises to Abraham?

9. How does Abraham's descendant Jesus bring this blessing to all people?

 ## To finish

If someone were to ask you about your most famous ancestor, on what basis could you answer that it is Abraham? What does it mean to be a child of Abraham today?

 ## Give thanks and pray

- Thank God that we can be included in Abraham's family and so receive the blessings of righteousness and the Spirit by trusting in Jesus.
- Ask God to help you be a blessing to the people around you by sharing with them the news of Jesus death so that they too can become members of Abraham's family by faith in Christ.

4. DAVID: THE KING OF ISRAEL

 Getting started

> The book of the genealogy of Jesus Christ, the son of David, the son of Abraham... So all the generations from Abraham to David were fourteen generations, and from David to the deportation to Babylon fourteen generations, and from the deportation to Babylon to the Christ fourteen generations. (Matt 1:1, 17)

Who are the greatest leaders in the history of your nation? What made these leaders great?

⚜ Light from the Word

Read 2 Samuel 7:1-16.

1. What is the situation of David and his kingdom (v. 1)?

2. What does David want to do for God? Why do you think he wants to do this?

3. How does God respond to David's plans?

4. What does God promise David?

Read Acts 2:22-39.

5. According to Peter, what happened to David?

6. What did David say about the Christ (God's promised king)?

7. How does Jesus' resurrection prove that he is the Christ?

8. What are the benefits for Peter's listeners of Jesus being the Christ (vv. 38-39)?

9. Where in Peter's sermon do you see particular echoes of 2 Samuel 7?

 ## To finish

Why would someone have Jesus as their ruler? If Jesus is already your ruler, how should the picture of him presented in these passages affect the way you think and live?

 ## Give thanks and pray

- Thank God that he fulfilled his promise to David to make one of David's descendants the ruler for all time when he raised Jesus from the dead.
- Thank God for this gift of his Spirit that Jesus, the son of David, now gives to his people.
- Ask God to help you live under the rule of King Jesus, guided by his Spirit.

5. RETURN FROM EXILE

 **Getting started**

The book of the genealogy of Jesus Christ, the son of David, the son of Abraham... So all the generations from Abraham to David were fourteen generations, and from David to the deportation to Babylon fourteen generations, and from the deportation to Babylon to the Christ fourteen generations. (Matt 1:1, 17)

What are your goals and aspirations for the future? What shapes these hopes? How are these hopes shaping your actions in the present?

☀ Light from the Word

Read Ezekiel 36:16-30.

1. What is the situation of the people Ezekiel is addressing?

2. Why are they in this position?

3. What things does God promise to do for Israel?

Read Ezekiel 37:1-14.

4. What will happen to the people to end the exile?

5. How would the exiles have felt when they received these promises?

Read Acts 1:1-8.

6. What are the apostles looking forward to and hoping for?

7. How does Jesus respond to their expectations?

8. What will be their mission?

9. How does this fulfil Old Testament expectations about Israel's return from exile and the restoration of God's kingdom? How might it have challenged some expectations?

 ## To finish

Think back to our opening question. How should the realities we have looked at in this study shape your aspirations for the future and your actions in the present?

 ## Give thanks and pray

- Thank God that he ended the exile of his people from himself when he raised Jesus from the dead and gave his Spirit to his people.
- Ask God to help you long for his kingdom and to be people who live consistently with the gift of the kingdom, his Spirit.

6. THE DEATH OF JESUS

 Getting started

> For I delivered to you as of first importance what I also received: that Christ died for our sins in accordance with the Scriptures and that he was buried. (1 Cor 15:3-4a)

How are relationships between people restored in today's world? What makes reconciliation successful or unsuccessful? What would it take to restore humanity's relationship with God?

💡 Light from the Word

Read Leviticus 4:27-35.

1. What process are the Israelites to follow for making sacrifices when they realize they have sinned?

2. What is the purpose of laying the hand on the animal's head (vv. 29, 33)?

3. What is achieved by the death of the animal?

4. What will this process teach Israel about how God views their sin?

Read Hebrews 9:24-28.

5. Where has Jesus appeared? What is the purpose of his appearing?

6. How has Jesus dealt with our sin?

7. When did Jesus make this sacrifice once for all?

8. What does this passage tell us about how God views our sin?

9. Despite our sin, how does this passage give us hope and encouragement?

 To finish

What are some practical ways in which we can respond to the knowledge that Jesus' death for our sins restores our relationship with God?

 Give thanks, confess and pray

- Thank God for sending Jesus to die for our sins and so pay the penalty of death for us that our sins deserved.
- Confess your sins to God and ask him to forgive you on the basis of Jesus' death.
- Ask God to transform you so that you live with him as your king.

7. THE RESURRECTION OF JESUS

 Getting started

> For I delivered to you as of first importance what I also received: that Christ... was raised on the third day in accordance with the Scriptures, and that he appeared to Cephas, then to the twelve. (1 Cor 15:3-5)

What is it that gives you joy and certainty in life? Is it possible to have certainty about the future? Why, or why not?

☀ Light from the Word

Read Psalm 16.

1. What is David asking God for (v. 1)?

2. How will God preserve him:

   • in life (vv. 7-8)?

   • in death (vv. 9-11)?

3. What is David's response to God, and to his God-given security?

Read Acts 13:32-41.

4. These verses are part of a sermon preached by the apostle Paul in the city of Antioch. According to Paul, how have the promises of God to Israel been fulfilled?

5. How, and by whom, was Psalm 16 ultimately fulfilled? How can we know this?

6. What are the consequences of Jesus' resurrection?

7. What warning does Paul give as he concludes his sermon? How might this warning be applicable to people today?

 To finish

How should our knowledge of Jesus' resurrection and its consequences affect us? How should it affect the way we think about our future?

 Give thanks and pray

- Thank God for Jesus' resurrection that fulfils God's promises, brings us forgiveness, gives us assurance and provides us with joy.
- Ask God to strengthen your faith in Jesus' resurrection so that you might be confidently joyful in the Lord.

8. THE PRESENT RULE OF JESUS

 Getting started

> Christ Jesus is the one who died—more than that, who was raised—who is at the right hand of God, who indeed is interceding for us. (Rom 8:34)

Who is the most powerful world ruler today? What makes them powerful? Who gave them this power?

💡 Light from the Word

Read Psalm 110.

1. What will God ("the LORD") do for David's Lord (or 'master') in verse 1?

2. How will God do this (v. 2)? What is this image meant to convey?

3. How will the people respond to David's Lord (v. 3)?

4. What does this psalm show us about the identity and character of David's Lord?

Read Hebrews 1:1-14.

5. Make a brief note of the various things God's Son has done for his people.

6. How is Jesus' present location a fulfilment of Psalm 110?

7. If the words of Psalm 110:1 are not addressed to the angels (v. 13), then to whom are they addressed?

8. Why do you think the author goes to such lengths to show the contrast between Jesus and the angels?

9. If Jesus is David's Lord from Psalm 110, then how should we think about his present rule in the world today?

 ## To finish

Who really rules our world? Look up Romans 13:1. How should we relate to the leaders of this world (Rom 13:1-2)?

Look back over this study, and briefly skim back over the previous studies. Of the truths you have learned about Jesus, which one brings you the most comfort and hope as you await his return?

 ## Give thanks and pray

- Thank God for his work in establishing Jesus as the ruler of the world.
- Ask God to help you to treat Jesus as the world ruler.
- Pray that our leaders (church and state) would be faithful servants of the Lord Jesus as they execute the power Jesus has given them (see 1 Tim 2:1-4).
- Pray also for those believers around the world who are undergoing persecution at the hands of evil leaders, that they would stand strong for the gospel and be faithful servants of the Lord Jesus.

FOR THE LEADER

What are Pathway Bible Guides?

The Pathway Bible Guides aim to provide simple, straightforward Bible study material for:

- Christians who are new to studying the Bible (perhaps because they've been recently converted or because they have joined a Bible study group for the first time)
- Christians who find other studies[1] too much of a stretch.

Accordingly, we've designed the studies to be short, straightforward and easy to use, with a simple vocabulary. At the same time, we've tried to do justice to the passages being studied, and to model good Bible-reading principles. We've tried to be simple without being simplistic; no-nonsense without being no-content.

The questions and answers assume a small group context, but it should be easy to adapt them to suit different situations, such as individual study and one-to-one.

Your role as leader

Because many in your group may not be used to reading and discussing a Bible passage in a group context, a greater level of responsibility will fall to you as the leader of the discussions. There are the usual responsibilities of preparation, prayer and managing group dynamics. In addition, there will be an extra dimension of forming and encouraging good Bible reading habits in people who may not have much of an idea of what those habits look like.

Questions have been kept deliberately brief and simple. For this reason, you may have to fill in some of the gaps that may have been addressed in, say, an Interactive Bible Study. Such 'filling in' may take the form of asking follow-up questions, or using your best judgement to work out when you might need to supply background information. That sort of information, and some suggestions about other questions you could ask, may be found in the following leader's notes. In addition, a *New Bible Dictionary* is always a useful aid to preparation, and simple commentaries such as those in the *Tyndale* or *Bible Speaks Today* series are often helpful. Consult these resources after you have done your own preparation.

On the question of background information, these studies are written from the assumption that God's word stands alone. God works through his Holy Spirit and the leaders he has gifted—such as you—to make his meaning clear. Assuming this to be true, the best interpreter and provider of background information for Scripture will not be academic historical research, but Scripture itself. Extra historical information may be useful for the purpose of illustration, but it is unnecessary for understanding and applying what God says to us.

The format of the studies

The discussion questions on each passage follow a simple pattern. There is a question at the beginning of each discussion that is intended to get people talking around the issues raised by the passage, and to give you some idea of how people are thinking. If the group turns out to be confident, motivated and comfortable with each other and the task at hand, you may even decide to skip this question.

Alternatively, if the group members are shy or quiet, you may decide to think of related types of questions that you could add in to the study, so as to maintain momentum in a non-threatening way.

After the first question, the remaining questions work through the passage sequentially, alternating between observation, interpretation and application in a way that will become obvious when you do your own preparation. The final question of each discussion, just before the opportunity for prayer, could be used in some groups to encourage (say) one person each week to give a short talk (it could be 1 minute or 5 minutes, depending on the topic and the people). The thinking here is that there's no better way to encourage understanding of a passage than to get people to the point where they can explain it to others. Use your judgement in making the best use of this final exercise each week, depending on the people in your group.

In an average group, it should be possible to work through the study in approximately 45 minutes. But it's important that you work out what your group is capable of, given the time available, and make adjustments accordingly. Work out in advance which questions or sub-points can be omitted if time is short. And have a few supplementary questions or discussion starters up your sleeve if your group is dealing with the material quickly and hungering for more. Each group is different. It's your job as leader to use the printed material as 'Bible Guides', and not as a set of questions that you must rigidly stick to regardless of your circumstances.

Preparation: 60/40/20

Ideally, group members should spend half an hour reading over the passage and pencilling in some answers *before* they come to the group. Not every group member will do this, of course, but encourage them with the idea that the more they prepare for the study, the more they will get out of the discussion.

In terms of your own preparation as leader, we recommend you put aside approximately *two hours*, either all at once or in two one-hour blocks, and that you divide up the time as follows:

- 60 minutes reading the passage and answering the questions yourself as best you can (without looking at the leader's notes or Bible commentaries)
- 40 minutes consulting the leader's notes (plus other resources, like commentaries). Add to your own answers, and jot down supplementary questions or other information that you want to have available as you lead the discussion. Make sure you write everything you need on the study pages—the last thing you want to do is to keep turning to the 'answers' in the back during the group discussion
- 20 minutes praying about the study and for your group members.

This 60/40/20 pattern will help you to focus on the Bible and what it's saying, rather than simply regurgitating to the group what is in the leader's notes. Remember, these notes are just that—notes to offer some help and guidance. They are not the Bible! As a pattern of preparation, 60/40/20 also helps you to keep praying for yourself and your group, that God would give spiritual growth as his word is sown in your hearts (see Luke 8:4-15; 1 Cor 3:5-7).

If, for some reason, you have less or more time to spend in preparation, simply apply the 60/40/20 proportions accordingly.

---

1. Such as the Interactive Bible Study (IBS) series also available from Matthias Media.

1. UNDERSTANDING JESUS

▶ **Remember 60/40/20**

 Getting started

People (mis)understand Jesus in many ways today. But this is not just a 21st-century phenomenon. Even in the first century many people misunderstood Jesus, particularly his death. We are told in 1 Corinthians 1:22-25 that Jews wanted miraculous signs and Greeks wanted wisdom, and so Jesus' death was a stumbling block to Jews and foolishness to Greeks.

The opening questions in our first study are designed to make people acknowledge that there are many (mis)understandings of Jesus. This should cause them to start thinking about the basis for their own understanding of Jesus. Since Christians hold that the death of Jesus is the power and wisdom of God, there is a lot at stake—indeed, our very salvation itself. But why do Christians think that Jesus' death is the power and wisdom of God? On what basis is this judgement made? These are the questions that this study aims to answer. The answer will then become the basis of the rest of the studies as we think about Jesus' life, death, resurrection and present rule.

Studying the passage

The questions from 1 Corinthians 15:1-8 are designed to demonstrate that Paul's gospel preaching has three components. First, Paul outlines the events of Jesus' life—his death, burial, resurrection and appearances. Second, these events have a particular significance: Jesus' death was "for our sins". Third, the reason Paul can attribute this significance to Jesus' death is because the Scriptures say so. Paul looks at these events through the glasses of the Scriptures, and so is able to explain their theological significance. In this context, "the Scriptures" are the writings of the Old Testament. Without these writings Paul would not have understood Jesus' death, just as the Greeks did not understand it because they were looking for something wise by human standards, and misguided Jews did not understand because they were looking for a miraculous sign. Hence, the basis for a right knowledge of Jesus is to understand him in light of the Old Testament.

The significance of this model for understanding Jesus must not be missed. The Corinthians (like all Christians since) are saved when they rightly understand the events of Jesus' death and resurrection—and this can only happen when the Old Testament is used as the interpretative key.

This point is reinforced in the reading and questions from Luke 24:13-49. In these verses the disciples do not understand that Jesus had to die and rise again, because they do not understand the Scriptures. On two occasions Luke tells us that their lack of understanding is removed when Jesus opens their minds to the Scriptures (vv. 27, 45), because it was the Old Testament Scriptures that foretold that the Christ would suffer, die and rise again on the third day.

When someone considers the Old Testament and then looks at Jesus, they will understand not only what happened to Jesus, but also its significance for themselves.

 # To finish

The closing questions reinforce the main point that we understand Jesus properly only in light of the Old Testament. This is significant because it is what makes or breaks our understanding of Jesus, and thus our salvation.

 # Give thanks and pray

At the end of each study you will find a few suggestions of things to give thanks for and pray about. It might also be a good place to think and pray for non-believing friends and family who misunderstand Jesus because they do not come to him through the eyes of Scripture.

2. THE HISTORY AND EXPECTATIONS OF ISRAEL

▶ Remember 60/40/20

 Getting started

This study investigates the birth of Jesus as recorded for us in Matthew's Gospel. Jesus was not born into a society that had no expectations, but into one that was waiting for a saviour. The opening questions raise the issue of national expectations in order to help people feel the situation into which Jesus was born. Some people will have particular expectations that will help them empathize with the situation described in Matthew 1-2. However, some will have few or no expectations for their nation's future, and the questions will help them see the difference between their perspective and that of Matthew 1-2. This difference will then open up a point of learning, as group members see the need to feel and listen to Israel's expectations, in order to better understand Jesus.

Studying the passage

While the study covers a large amount of material, the passages work together with the same logic to make one overall point: the events of Jesus' birth happened to fulfil the expectations of the Old Testament.

The questions on the genealogy (Matt 1:1-17) are intended to help people see that Jesus is a descendant of Abraham (the father of Israel) and David (the greatest king of Israel). These two men and their relationships with Jesus are the focus of the next two studies. Further, Jesus is born into a nation in exile—a nation that is captive to others and is longing for restoration as a nation in their own right (this is the focal point of our fifth study).

As you work through the various sections of Matthew, note that the promises from the Old Testament gave rise to particular expectations among the people.

In most cases, the first question asks about the event itself, while subsequent questions show that the reason for the event is the fulfilment of Old Testament expectation. So Jesus is born to the virgin Mary to fulfil the prophecy of Isaiah 7:14; he is born in Bethlehem to fulfil Micah 5:2; and Joseph takes Jesus to Egypt to fulfil Hosea 11:1. In this last case, Jesus fulfils the Old Testament prophecy in a way that is quite different to the original context (where the nation of Israel was leaving slavery in Egypt), showing that the fulfilment of prophecy is not simplistic, and that these events still find their ultimate fulfilment in Jesus.

Even the shocking events of Herod killing the male children in Bethlehem fulfil Old Testament prophecy (Jer 31:15). The last expectation—that Jesus will live in Nazareth, allowing him to be called a Nazarene—does not fulfil any specific prophecy. Nazareth was a despised area of Israel, and what is on view here is a theme taught in the prophets: that the Christ would be despised (cf. Pss 22:6-8, 13; 69:8, 20-21; Isa 11:1; 49:7; 53:2-3, 8; Dan 9:26). Note that unlike the other Old Testament passages quoted in Matthew 1-2, this saying is attributed to "the prophets", not a specific prophet.

To finish

This section is a review of the material read and discussed in Matthew 1-2. It aims to reinforce the pattern that sees the events of Jesus' life as occurring in order to fulfil the history and expectations of Israel. This history and these expectations come from the prophets, as they spoke for God. This helps to lay the foundation for our more detailed examination of the Old Testament in upcoming studies.

3. ABRAHAM: THE FATHER OF ISRAEL

▶ Remember 60/40/20

 ## Getting started

Having someone (in)famous in your family can often be a point of pride or despair. Their actions may have shaped you—your values, where you live, etc. By raising this subject, the opening questions prepare people to examine the founding father of Israel—the man Abraham. God's promises to Abraham and Abraham's subsequent trust in God started the nation of Israel and shaped the Israelites' understanding of themselves and the world.

Studying the passage

The opening questions from Genesis 12 draw attention to God's promises to Abraham. These promises of becoming a great nation, being blessed, and being a blessing to all people on earth were partially fulfilled in the nation of Israel. However, when we reach the New Testament, Israel is captive to the Romans and effectively in exile from God. But Israel still holds expectations of God restoring these promises; of the Israelites once again being a great nation whom God blesses, making them in turn a blessing to all peoples on earth.

The questions from Galatians reveal that God has fulfilled his promises to Abraham in Abraham's descendent, Jesus. It is by believing (or faith) that someone becomes a child of Abraham (v. 7). Abraham's trust, or faith, in God's ability to keep his promises resulted in God counting righteousness to Abraham (v. 6). The blessings that Abraham's children (both Jew and Gentile) receive are justification (v. 8) and the gift of the Spirit (v. 14). Because it is by faith and not by birth that someone becomes a child of Abraham, all the nations of the earth are blessed. The contrast between those who are "cursed" (those who "rely on works of the law") and those who are blessed (those who "live by faith") shows the importance of faith even more clearly.

However, it is not just 'having faith' that makes someone a child of Abraham. We can (and do) have faith in all sorts of things. Abraham's faith was in God's ability to keep his promises. In many ways our faith is similar to Abraham's, but it is slightly different: it is no longer in God's ability to fulfil his promises in the future, but in the one who has come and fulfilled them (vv. 13-14). Jesus' death on a tree (a metaphor for the cross) means that Jesus took the punishment we deserve for our sins—the curse of the law—so that we can be justified (declared not guilty). We have been redeemed from the law's curse so that we are able to receive the blessing of God's Spirit.

To finish

This section reviews the material about Abraham by asking people to think of themselves as children of Abraham. If they were unable to give an answer about someone famous in their family, they should now have an answer! If they spoke about someone famous (or infamous) among their ancestors, they should now be able to see that Abraham is more significant, since being his child means sharing in the blessings of justification and the Spirit.

4. DAVID: THE KING OF ISRAEL

▶ Remember 60/40/20

 Getting started

Our nations and our personal identities are strongly affected by the leaders of our nations. The opening questions are aimed to get people thinking about their leaders and why they have the power and influence that they have. These questions introduce the key theme of this study: leadership. The questions open up the issue so that when David and Jesus are examined, it is natural to think about them in terms of their leadership and the reasons they were (and are) great leaders.

Studying the passage

The first set of questions from 2 Samuel 7 focuses on David. As the passage starts, David's kingdom is at rest and the people have security in the land (vv. 1, 11). While enjoying the benefits of this rest, David perceives that God does not have the same security—he lives in a tent, not a house or a temple. So David determines to build a 'house' for God to live in amongst the people. God hears David's plans and sends the prophet Nathan, who brings God's words to David. God says that it will not be David who builds a house for God, but one of David's descendants. Instead, God will build a house for David, or more than a house—a dynasty, appointing one of David's descendants to rule forever (v. 16).

Solomon, David's son, does build the house for God (the temple), but as his kingship progresses, he becomes increasingly rebellious. The kings subsequent to Solomon keep the family name alive, but fail to fulfil the promise. The Old Testament ends with the people of Israel looking for the promised king—the king descended from David who would restore the nation and rule forever.

The second set of questions examine Peter's first sermon in Acts 2. He explains why the apostles are speaking in tongues—it is the result of the gift of God's Spirit. At the crucial point in his sermon, Peter refers to David. He notes that David died and was buried in a tomb that the people could identify (v. 29). Yet David knew the promise of God about one of his descendants ruling, and he spoke about how we could identify this man—by his physical resurrection (vv. 31-32). The Christ would be resurrected from the grave, and his body would not see decay (vv. 25-28, 31-32). Peter then identifies Jesus as this man, the one who fulfils God's promise to David. Jesus is the descendant of David, the Christ, who reigns forever. The benefits to his people of Jesus being the Christ are the gift of the Spirit (vv. 33, 38) and the forgiveness of sin (v. 38).

 ## To finish

This section reviews the material about David by asking people to consider why someone would have Jesus as their ruler. We have just seen that the resurrection is the key event that marks Jesus as worthy to be God's promised ruler. Further, we also saw that the direct benefits of Jesus being the ruler are the gift of the Spirit and forgiveness of sin. Taken together, the reality of the resurrection and the gifts of the Spirit and forgiveness are the reasons why people should have Jesus as their ruler. This section is therefore a good opportunity to encourage people to think about whether Jesus is their Lord and King, and how following this king should shape their lives.

5. RETURN FROM EXILE

▶ Remember 60/40/20

 ## Getting started

We all have plans and goals for our futures: they may be related to family (spouse, children), finances (career, house) or fun (holiday). Our aspirations for the future will inevitably shape what we do in the present: we save for a house, we study for a career, or we date to find a spouse. If we are planning to run a marathon, we train in the lead-up to the race. These opening questions are designed to get us thinking about our situation in life, what things shape our aspirations and values, and how our future goals then shape our lives in the present. As we start thinking about the biblical concept of the exile, we need to understand that the people of Israel had received particular promises from God that shaped their vision of the future.

Studying the passage

The first set of questions from Ezekiel 36:16-30 aims to help us understand the situation of the people in exile and the reasons for their exile. God's people had disobeyed his commands, so God had brought the Babylonians in judgement against them in around 586 BC (God's judgement on the people's sin had been prophesied back in Deuteronomy 28). The Babylonians destroyed Jerusalem and carried the people off into exile in the land of Babylon. However, now that the people are in exile, God promises to restore them and bring them back to the land of Israel. He promises to change their hearts of stone, which made them disobedient and sinful, and to give them new hearts and a new Spirit, his Spirit, which will enable them to be obedient once more (vv. 26-27).

The second reading from Ezekiel 37:1-14 paints a picture of what will happen to bring about these promises of restoration and the gift of the Spirit. In exile Israel is dead, like a pile of dried bones. For the Israelites to be restored, they need to be resurrected and given the life-giving Spirit of God. So the resurrection and the gift of the Spirit are what will precede and indicate the re-establishment of God's people as a nation and as a kingdom. It's helpful to note that the Hebrew word for 'Spirit' (*ruach*) is the same as the word for 'breath' or 'wind'.

The following section of Ezekiel (37:15-27) picks up the theme of kingdom more explicitly, so may be worth referring to if time allows (especially verse 24).

When we get to the New Testament, we meet Israel in spiritual exile. They might be physically living in the Promised Land, but the promised resurrection has not occurred and the Spirit has not been poured out. God's kingdom, for which they long, has not yet been established (cf. Luke 2:25-26, 36-38). Given this context, it is understandable that the apostles are eagerly anticipating the restoration of the kingdom (Acts 1:6). They have just witnessed Jesus' resurrection, which, according to Ezekiel, will precede the coming of the kingdom.

The third reading picks up on this sense of anticipation and explores what the death and resurrection of Jesus mean in the situation. The apostles are looking forward to the restoration of the kingdom to Israel because Jesus has just spent 40 days appearing to them, proving that he has been raised from the dead and speaking about the kingdom of God (v. 3). However, the other thing that Ezekiel promised would precede the kingdom (the giving of the Spirit) has not yet taken place, so the apostles are told to wait for it (vv. 4-5, 8).

Once they have the Spirit, they are to testify to Jesus' resurrection throughout the whole earth (v. 8). Their mission will be to tell everyone that God has fulfilled his Old Testament promises to restore his kingdom. The resurrection of Jesus is the first indicator, and the second is his gift of the Spirit to his people, bringing them back to life to live in obedience to him.

To finish

This section asks people to consider their hopes and aspirations in light of the knowledge of Jesus' resurrection and gift of the Spirit. We now live in the age where the kingdom is restored, but where Jesus has not yet returned to make this publicly visible to all. This reality should shape our lives more than anything else does. We should be people who follow the Spirit and are obedient to God as we await his return.

6. THE DEATH OF JESUS

▶ Remember 60/40/20

 Getting started

This study focuses on the death of Jesus for our sins as the way in which God restores our relationship with himself. In order to prepare people to think about Jesus' death, the opening questions are designed to get people discussing how reconciliation is achieved today. We all have relational problems with others at various times in our lives—how do we go about fixing these problems? The final question narrows in on the issue covered in the study: how can our relationship with God be fixed? This sets the background for considering the issues of sacrifice and atonement.

Studying the passage

The aim of this section is to investigate how the New Testament understands the death of Jesus in the light of the Old Testament's teaching about sin.

The first set of questions, from Leviticus 4:27-35, displays the Israelites' understanding of how sin is dealt with and atonement is achieved. God gives explicit directions to the people that when they sin they are to bring an offering (a goat or a lamb) to the temple, which will die for their sin. The sinner is to lay their hand on the head of the animal, identifying themselves with it, and then kill the animal for their sin, in their place. The priest is to then take the blood of the dead animal and present it to God by smearing it over the altar. The fat of the animal is to be removed and burned up. This process will make atonement for the sinner and they will be forgiven. By this process, the Israelites will learn that the punishment for sin is death, and the way to avoid the consequences of sin is to sacrifice an animal in their place. The entire system will also impress upon them the grave seriousness of their sin, by showing them that atonement requires the shedding of blood and can only be achieved by following the process instituted by God himself.

The second set of questions focuses in on one passage in the New Testament where this understanding of sin and its consequences is discussed. In the New Testament, Jesus takes the place of the animal and the priest. So in Hebrews 9:24-28, Jesus enters the heavenly temple to appear before God as our priest, on our behalf. He appears in order to put away sin by the sacrifice of himself—that is, by his death for sin on our behalf. He was offered once for all to take the penalty for our sin in our place (to bear the sins of many; v. 28). He died in our place to make atonement with God for our sins. This happened in accordance with the Old Testament teaching (seen in passages like Leviticus 4) that the penalty for sin is death—a penalty that was formerly paid by the death of animals, but which is now paid by the death of Jesus. Other passages that make this explicit include Hebrews 9:11-14 and 10:11-14, and 1 John 1:5-2:2.

To finish

This question aims to draw together the various parts of the study and prompt people to think about their response to the good news of restored relationship with God because of the death of Jesus for sin. Some possible answers include:

- confess our sin
- ask God for forgiveness
- be certain of our salvation when we doubt
- be confident in prayer that we are now able to approach God without fear because of our restored relationship with him.

7. THE RESURRECTION OF JESUS

▶ Remember 60/40/20

 Getting started

This study investigates Jesus' resurrection and its implications for us. We will see that Jesus' resurrection fulfils God's promises, brings us forgiveness, gives us assurance, and provides us with joy. So to get the study started, the opening questions raise the issues of certainty and joy. It is important to allow people to express the joy and certainty they get from things in life (family, friends, etc.), because God created all things good and for our benefit. But it is also worthwhile to get people thinking about the transitory nature of these earthly things, and so open up the way for people to see that real assurance and joy is found as a result of the resurrection.

Studying the passage

The opening few questions based on Psalm 16 are designed to show that the resurrection is God's means of preserving his anointed king. David asks God to preserve him (v. 1) and God does this in life by providing his word, and in death by the resurrection of his body. God keeps David safe, showing him how to live as he was designed to live (vv. 7-8). When death finally does overcome his body, God promises to not let David's body decay, but to raise him from the dead (v. 10). This gives David enormous joy and confidence about his present and future (v. 11). Yet David did die and his body did see decay—so what is the psalm talking about?

The New Testament provides the answer, as it interprets this psalm as referring to Jesus. The verses in Acts 13 teach that God fulfilled his promises to the nation of Israel when he raised Jesus from the dead. Jesus is the descendant of David whose body did not see decay. We know this because he was physically raised from the dead, and he appeared to the apostles and to many others (1 Corinthians 15:5-8 provides a list of people to whom Jesus appeared). The job of the apostles in Acts is to bear witness to Jesus' resurrection (1:8), as it is the means of forgiveness (13:38). Psalm 16 is also integral to the sermon in Acts 2, where the same logic is evident. David spoke of Jesus' physical resurrection in the psalm, and in Acts 2 Jesus' resurrection fulfils these promises and leads to the gift of the Spirit and the forgiveness of sins.

To finish

It is one thing to understand that Jesus was physically raised from the dead. It is another to see the implications of this for how we act and feel now. The aim of this section is to review the consequences of the resurrection as outlined in Psalm 16 and in Acts 13. David's response to God's promise of the resurrection was confidence and joy. This should also be part of our response—in fact, our response should be even stronger than David's, because the resurrection is now something that has happened in the past. It is not just a promise awaiting fulfilment; it is a completed historical reality to be celebrated. In Jesus, God has given us a 'case study' to prove beyond doubt that resurrection will happen to everyone in the future.

Further, Jesus' resurrection in particular fulfils God's promises and brings forgiveness of sins. As a result, we should be people who have confidence before God and certainty for the future, allowing us to be filled with joy. This joy is not based on things of this world, but on a past event in this world that ensures what will happen in the future.

8. THE PRESENT RULE OF JESUS

▶ Remember 60/40/20

 ## Getting started

This study examines the significance of Jesus' present rule. It builds on Psalm 110, in which David speaks of his Lord—the one to whom God will subject the world. When we turn to the New Testament we see that Jesus is this ruler, and that the present world is subject to Jesus. So the opening questions are to get us thinking about who rules the world from a human perspective, and how these rulers came into their positions. The aim here is to provoke thought about human rulers, which will enable us to properly appreciate that Jesus is the one true ruler of the world—the one who gives these human leaders their power, and the one to whom these human rulers must give account.

Studying the passage

The questions from Psalm 110 introduce the concept that God ("the LORD") will appoint his ruler (David's Lord). One of the difficulties modern readers experience when they encounter this psalm is misunderstanding the translation procedure of many English Bibles. When God's proper name (Yahweh) is translated in the Old Testament, instead of translating it as 'Yahweh', it is translated as 'LORD' all in capitals. This can become confusing when the word 'Lord' (in lowercase letters) also occurs, as is the case in Psalm 110:1. So the opening verse records the speech of Yahweh to David's Lord (or 'master'). This psalm, then, records the words of God to someone who rules over David. God promises that this person will sit at his right hand, and that he, God, will subdue all this person's enemies. God will do this through the use of force (v 2), and the people will freely offer themselves in service to David's Lord (v. 3). In the end, David's Lord will judge the earth with power and conquer his enemies (vv. 5-7). The question, then, is: who is this person? Who is David's Lord (cf. Matt 22:41-46)?

Again, the New Testament provides the answer to these questions, as Psalm 110 is used to understand Jesus' present rule of the world. Jesus is David's Lord, the one to whom God was speaking. The aim of the questions from Hebrews 1 is to help us see how this psalm is used to understand Jesus as David's Lord. We have already seen that Jesus provided purification for the sins of his people by his death on their behalf (v. 3). Hebrews 1 takes the story a little further: once Jesus had provided purification for sin, he sat down at the right hand of God in heaven (v. 3). This picks up the imagery of the psalm, where David's Lord is called by God to sit at his right hand (Ps 110:1). So Jesus is presently sitting at God's right hand in heaven. Following the thought of the psalm, God is now subduing Jesus' enemies, his people are offering themselves freely in his service, and Jesus will come again to judge.

In Hebrews 1:5-14, the absolute power and authority of Jesus are highlighted through a series of comparisons with the angels. For example, God has never spoken to any of his angels as if they were his Son (v. 5), but he has spoken this way of Jesus (e.g. Matt 3:17). Further, God speaks of this Son being worshipped by the angels; it is their job to serve him (cf. Luke 2:9-14), and the Son is given the sceptre of the kingdom (Heb 1:8-9). To summarize and complete this idea, the author of Hebrews quotes Psalm 110:1 directly and notes that these words were not said to angels but were addressed to Jesus (Heb 1:13), who is greater than any angel. So God has appointed Jesus as his Son to sit at his right hand and rule the world. Jesus is David's Lord who presently rules our world.

 ## To finish

This section reviews the study by asking people to consider the relationship between the real ruler of the world (Jesus) and our human leaders. The Romans passage points us to the way we should relate to our human leaders as envoys of Jesus—with respect and obedience. This may raise some situational questions about what to do when the rulers are promoting ways of living that are contrary to Jesus' word, so it is a good opportunity to make a list of things we should be praying for our leaders. It also opens a wider opportunity for prayer, as we can pray for other Christians around the world who may be subjected to the leadership of cruel or oppressive leaders.

But ultimately, even in the face of sometimes evil earthly governments, the absolute goodness and supremacy of the Son—David's Lord (as seen not just in this study, but throughout the entire series)—is cause for enormous comfort and rejoicing for all who trust in him.

Feedback on this resource

We really appreciate getting feedback about our resources—not just suggestions for how to improve them, but also positive feedback and ways they can be used. We especially love to hear that the resources may have helped someone in their Christian growth.

You can send feedback to us via the 'Feedback' menu in our online store, or write to us at PO Box 225, Kingsford NSW 2032, Australia.

Matthias Media is an evangelical publishing ministry that seeks to persuade all Christians of the truth of God's purposes in Jesus Christ as revealed in the Bible, and equip them with high-quality resources, so that by the work of the Holy Spirit they will:

- abandon their lives to the honour and service of Christ in daily holiness and decision-making
- pray constantly in Christ's name for the fruitfulness and growth of his gospel
- speak the Bible's life-changing word whenever and however they can—in the home, in the world and in the fellowship of his people.

It was in 1988 that we first started pursuing this mission, and in God's kindness we now have more than 300 different ministry resources being used all over the world. These resources range from Bible studies and books through to training courses and audio sermons.

To find out more about our large range of very useful resources, and to access samples and free downloads, visit our website:

www.matthiasmedia.com

How to buy our resources

1. Direct from us over the internet:
   - in the US: www.matthiasmedia.com
   - in Australia and the rest of the world: www.matthiasmedia.com.au

2. Direct from us by phone:
   - in the US: 1 866 407 4530
   - in Australia: 1300 051 220
   - international: +61 2 9233 4627

> Register at our website for our **free** regular email update to receive information about the latest new resources, **exclusive special offers**, and free articles to help you grow in your Christian life and ministry.

3. Through a range of outlets in various parts of the world. Visit **www.matthiasmedia.com/contact** for details about recommended retailers in your part of the world, including www.thegoodbook.co.uk in the United Kingdom.

4. Trade enquiries can be addressed to:
   - in the US and Canada: sales@matthiasmedia.com
   - in Australia and the rest of the world: sales@matthiasmedia.com.au

Pathway Bible Guides

Pathway Bible Guides are simple, straightforward, easy-to-read Bible studies, ideal for groups who are new to studying the Bible, or groups with limited time for study. We've designed the studies to be short and easy to use, with an uncomplicated vocabulary. At the same time, we've tried to do justice to the passages being studied, and to model good Bible-reading principles. Pathway Bible Guides are simple without being simplistic; no-nonsense without being no-content.

FOR MORE INFORMATION OR TO ORDER CONTACT:

Matthias Media	Matthias Media (USA)
Ph: 1300 051 220	Ph: 1 866 407 4530
Int: +61 2 9233 4627	Int: +1 330 953 1702
Email: sales@matthiasmedia.com.au	Email: sales@matthiasmedia.com
www.matthiasmedia.com.au	www.matthiasmedia.com

Interactive Bible Studies

Interactive Bible Studies are a bit like a guided tour of a famous city. They take you through a particular part of the Bible, helping you to know where to start, pointing out things along the way, suggesting avenues for further exploration, and making sure that you know how to get home. Like any good tour, the real purpose is to allow you to go exploring for yourself—to dive in, have a good look around, and discover for yourself the riches that God's word has in store.

In other words, these studies aim to provide stimulation and input and point you in the right direction, while leaving you to do plenty of the exploration and discovery yourself.

We pray that these studies will stimulate lots of 'interaction'—interaction with the Bible, with the things we've written, with your own current thoughts and attitudes, with other people as you discuss them, and with God as you talk to him about it all.

FOR MORE INFORMATION OR TO ORDER CONTACT:

Matthias Media
Ph: 1300 051 220
Int: +61 2 9233 4627
Email: sales@matthiasmedia.com.au
www.matthiasmedia.com.au

Matthias Media (USA)
Ph: 1 866 407 4530
Int: +1 330 953 1702
Email: sales@matthiasmedia.com
www.matthiasmedia.com

Guidebooks for Life

Some Christian books are all theory and no practical application; others are all stories and tips with no substance. The Guidebooks for Life series aims to achieve a vital balance—that is, to dig into the Bible and discover what God is telling us there, as well as applying that truth to our daily Christian lives.

We want this series of books to grow into a basic library for every Christian, covering all the important topics and issues of the Christian life in an accessible, straightforward way.

As of December 2012, the series contains the following titles:
- Defending the Gospel
- Encouragement: How Words Change Lives
- Faith
- A Foot in Two Worlds
- Guidance and the Voice of God
- Keep the Faith: Shift your thinking on doubt
- One Forever: The transforming power of being in Christ
- Prayer and the Voice of God
- A Sinner's Guide to Holiness
- Suffering Well

FOR MORE INFORMATION OR TO ORDER CONTACT:

Matthias Media
Ph: 1300 051 220
Int: +61 2 9233 4627
Email: sales@matthiasmedia.com.au
www.matthiasmedia.com.au

Matthias Media (USA)
Ph: 1 866 407 4530
Int: +1 330 953 1702
Email: sales@matthiasmedia.com
www.matthiasmedia.com